Journey of a Whitefeather

"Remove my mask… write my story"

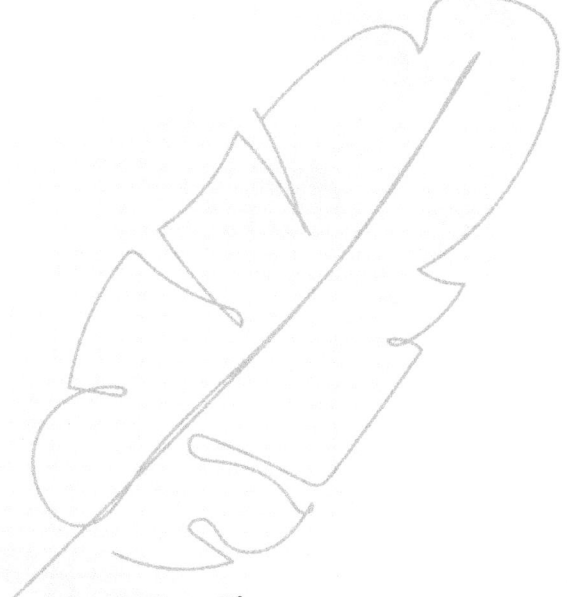

Steve Clogstoun
B.App.Sci (PhysED) / Dip.Ed
Ad.Dip Health Science (Myotherapy)

First published by Busybird Publishing 2024

Copyright © 2024 Journey of a Whitefeather ®

ISBN: 978-0-646-88303-8

This book is copyright. Apart from any fair dealing for the purposes of study, research, criticism, review, or as otherwise permitted under the Copyright Act, no part may be reproduced by any process without written permission. Enquiries should be made through the publisher.

This is a work of fiction. Any similarities between places and characters are a coincidence.

Administration and Production by Mr. Graeme Smith.

Cover image: Real People Victoria Talent Agency

Photos: Ursala Hill, Jaylee Dixon @rockumentalmusic, Wrestlerock

Edited by: Mr. Peter Symons

Cover design: Busybird Publishing

Layout and typesetting: Busybird Publishing

Busybird Publishing
2/118 Para Road
Montmorency, Victoria
Australia 3094
www.busybird.com.au

Email : whitewarriorhealth@gmail.com
https://linktr.ee/wwhjourneyofawhitefeather
Ph : 0427185185

This book is dedicated to:

*Sahara-Rose, my rock through all the times,
good and bad,
I love you.*

In dedication to:

*Tara, Michael, George (Lord Lush),
Nek (The Firestarter), "Dom", Bruno,
Pauline, Danny, Coby, Ann and Sue.*

Foreword

The Story behind the Story

My name is Steve Clogstoun, well that's my birth name, but everyone knows me as Jay and I am motivational speaker & mentor, physical education teacher, natural healer and author, and someone who has a love for life.

Apparently I have this contagious energy that could be considered crazy to some, but to the people who know me, it's my greatest superpower.

When we are brought into the world, we wish it to be greatest time of our lives. We meet people, we fall in love, we travel around the world, and we find ourselves and our purpose.

Let's look at what happens and how we learn the hardest lessons.

It all started in Western Australia, more specifically Fremantle, has been my spiritual home since I made my first trip there in 1995. As I stepped off the train at Fremantle I felt I was home. The people, the places, the energy, it was the most beautiful feeling. I walked the streets, with the smile on my face and just enjoyed every step I took, feeling home.

I live in Melbourne, on the south coast of Australia, and you may ask how weird it is that I state that Fremantle is my home.

Since I was 7 years old I watched the State of Origin football — Western Australia versus Victoria. There was no doubt that I would barrack for the 'Sandgropers' with the great Maurice Rioli leading the way. This is when I really missed home. It continues to this day.

So what does this have to do with *Journey of a Whitefeather*?

Let's put it this way. When a white feather drops at your feet after you change you stage name to Jay Whitefeather, you know that's a sign.

Where I am in my life at the moment, I can say that I am coming into my journey and the purpose I wield. I am very proud of each of these and it has been a lot of work but in saying that we all have it in us to do what I have done. We grow and take things that become so significant to us, we don't realize it's just one skill or teaching that will shape you into the person you have always wanted to be. In 1996, I was very privileged to run my own natural healing business — Positive Health Massage — which is now called White Warrior Health, worked for various professional sporting clubs and lectured at various natural therapy colleges and TAFEs around Victoria. I am just finding out that this was only the start of my journey. Over the last 12 years, I was an Australian heavyweight champion professional wrestler, which I had to retire from due to a major back injury, I went back to university, and I was a single dad to my young child. This has been my biggest life lesson. I had to be more, and I had to get my life back on track which meant to get a degree as a teacher and settle into a school and let life go on. This was an important foundational decision to make and the right one I will say, but I had more to learn and give to myself and the world. After retiring from wrestling, I started DDPYoga, a fitness system started by former 3-time world champion professional wrestler Diamond Dallas Page (www.ddpy.com) because my body had broken down. After working hard for 8 years I became the first DDPY qualified instructor in Australasia.

I completed my degree in physical education with second class honours. One of the greatest gifts I received was the amount of work I did with underprivileged children and children with a disability. The number of skills I learnt working with wonderful teachers and seeing people for what they are and what I could do to enhance their lives in some little way was awe inspiring.

The next stage of my life was interesting. I met a number of magnificent individuals that changed my life and made me into the person I always wanted to be. Again, they opened me up to special gifts and some damaged goods that were inside me. I now know it was the battle with my past and became the path to my Oz. I always say the yellow brick road is where we all wish to be and have superpowers to make our lives better. I know now it was in me, I just needed to be safe to believe in what gifts I have to offer the world and grow as a human being.

I went through a rough time from 2019 to 2020. I suffered with some emotional stress that was revealed to be past traumas. It was hard not being able to get up sometimes, fighting the good versus bad in your head, acting each day and not feeling worthy. The invisible boy, not heard, not seen and even to me I know that for decades I was hiding my pain and ashamed to be me. I suffered through major anxiety and stress-related medical problems culminating in being admitted to hospital. I thank the beautiful people who helped me that day.

I had medical tests and to my horror they were treating me as a possible stroke victim. My heart sunk and I was just scared, plain and simple. In the months leading up to that moment I didn't realize the hurt I was going through and how I tried to stop the pain. You don't know yourself until you look back at the past and just shake your head and think, 'What was I doing?', knowing you were just trying to get through life and the hard times. The hardest thing to do was to look at myself and see a person who has battled through life and had to make changes to become better. In every sense in my life, I had to look at how and why I was the way I was. I had to be true to myself and my feelings, but also love me.

What I found was lacking and non-existent in that way and I couldn't truly believe in myself because I didn't know how to, due to past hurt and programming. When you see the world through different eyes, the horizon looks so much different, through the eyes of your soul and protecting your spirit first. This is where the writings started and where it started was in my spiritual home —Fremantle, Western Australia. I understood personal development, believing in yourself and all that comes with it. It is great knowledge but when you're scared to be you, there is nothing that can help you until you can help yourself. I had definitely done a lot in my life, and I was proud, but the biggest battle was coming. I sought professional help which was the first step to opening up. I am grateful to my counsellor who assisted me in that stage of my life.

I could see what I was missing out on, but it was only until I met Greg Riley and Michael McNair who graciously invited me into the Shadow Warrior course that I began to develop. It showed me that I am important, and I have a lot more to give other with the superpowers I have. This course gave me the safety to be me with absolutely no judgement, something I feared and had brought into my life for decades. Healing and having the chance to feel safe to speak, grow and know that I am worthy, even in the darkest times. When pen hit the paper, the emotions poured forth.

I had thought to myself that this would cure everything, but I was I wrong, it was only the start of the newest stage of the education of my life and walking through the forbidden door. What is this you ask, it's the door to the deepest secrets of you, the key to finding the truest version of you and your purpose. I will say going through this door wasn't that hard, it was the emotions that were excreted from the deepest part of my soul were the hardest to deal with.

Lucky, I have very understanding friends who helped me through this time of life. I will mention here, if you believe that you were led or guided to a situation to assist in your growth, believe it, I can tell you. We are all here to learn lessons, well I believe this. I did this when I was in a situation where I had to step up for myself, say no I will not keep going the way it was, believe in what I am feeling within myself. The great thing is, I found myself circling in the same pattern I have been repeating for decades in different scenarios.

I will warn you, going through the forbidden door and into the forest of your deepest fears and worries, your shadow side will come forth. There was a little cage within my heart, that my deepest emotions and hurt has been kept under lock and key for decades. I believe I have allowed it to be opened. Now to this day I will be dealing with the contents, healing all and using the power to be a better person and greater human.

To cut a long story short, I learned about the values that I held, I understood the power of acceptance of others and where I have been on my journey, forgiveness and to understand that to become more you have to face your fears and walk strong and proud. It wasn't as simple as I have written in this book, but I am proud to say that I am on the way to happiness. Today I am gaining peace through my journey and my words so I can become the person have always wanted to be. I love writing and will continue to do so. I am always looking for readings and knowledge on various topics in the personal development field, a lot that I have read before, but with this new inner strength of character I can see it for more than what it is.

From my journey I believe I have what I call my 'Bat-Belt of Gifts', that have been gifted to me to help myself and others. So many new gifts come to me each day I am on this earth, I am so grateful I found this gift of writing and I have written my thoughts in poetry many times. In the times of hurt I found peace in the pen and paper. I also found my love for music, keeping as fit as possible, indulging back into my hobbies and the creativity that comes with playing piano and bass.

So I hope these verses help and teach you, and help you see inside someone who has loved life but who has walked the journey of life alone but found a place that he found that he calls home.

I am grateful for my friends, family and the people who have been there for me in my times of need. The people who believed in me when I didn't see the light within the shadows. There is always light within in your heart and sometimes you just need those few words or a look that just says, 'You are that beautiful person you feel inside'.

Thank you, Fremantle, all the people who have believed in me and to all the people who have stood up for me and beside me, I smile and shed a tear when I think what you mean to me.

My last words that I want to say. Always look for signs, be aware because the answers you want are sometimes right in front of you, thank you Cody. Stories have been written, stories have been talked about for centuries.

Now I remove my mask, and I write my story

"The process of discovery is painful because to do it right, to do it authentic, you will have to go to places you don't want to go"

Blackie Lawless of W.A.S.P.

"Be the best there is, the best there was and the best there ever will be"

Bret "Hitman" Hart, Former WWF Champion and current WWE Hall of Fame Inductee

Journey of a Whitefeather

A Message for all readers…

Published 30 August 2021

Thank you for my journey….. and thank you for being apart of this

To those who have taught me lessons and the ones who have been there to catch me. It's when I decide to walk into that deep forest and face the one enemy, me..

It all changed., and it continues to grow, only this time with awareness, forgiveness and love for all, especially me… because I am worthy, visible and valued. Is this a story, yes, it the messages and thoughts that I have. It's what you feel and what you write to allow healing.

If you read this, take heed of the words and take what lessons or messages it ignites in you. It may be the key to a journey that you have been waiting for, or a lesson you need to learn, or it is the answer you have been asking for…

… Embrace your hurt & heal gloves…

… Stay in the moment and embrace your flow of energy…

…Be aware of your vibration and protect that

…Stand up and face your shadow warrior…

…Remember your Sword of Values…

..Trust in the universe, the flow and yourself

Remember is it worth being right or being totally free and living your life… everyday I am getting better, but I still have a way to go, but the roller coaster I am on is flying now….

Now it's time to take that first step and let me motivate and guide you to your greatest gift … You.

Remove your Mask and write your story.

Journey of a Whitefeather Socials

Video / Audio Version of the Book

Chapter 1

Published 30 August 2021

**The long journey starts with one step…
the hardest decision I have ever made…**

Train whistle is blowing

A wild ride

Excitement is coming

The way we will live our lives

What's inside us

What's inside us

Our hearts desires

What make us tick

We've been through a storm

Now lets live

We have prepared

For these moments, the magic

Carried by the raven

As it flies past our carriage

I look and say
Oh mystical creature
Upon this new moon
What can you give me
It speaks to me
The other passengers
Look with delight
Magic is all around us
Don't worry about tomorrow
One step can make 1000
Do it, Do it now
In your mind put a plan out there
You are now worthy
It's time
The train passengers board again
Ready for a great trip
Under the new moon
With our goals in sight
You just use the magic of the raven
Believe in me believe in you

Chapter 2

Published 30 August 2021

Remember your worth and value… believe it, then live it….. You'll see the truth

Plants

Animals

Connection to spirit

Letting go

Forgetting to control tomorrow

It doesn't come

Today is here

Plan for tomorrow

Don't force the outcome

My message today

Enjoy today

I awake in the train

My friend looks at me

Good morning warrior

I say hello

With a bright smile

The clouds are above us

But I feel good

We go through times,

Times of change

Building strength

Building character

What do I want

A lot for me

But inner peace

Pure heart

Connection to spirit

Grateful for each breath

Happy

about the people around me

Increasing my aura

My mind is clear

Keep this feeling

Use the plants

The animals

2/3

Their medicine is helping, More than I know

Let the day begin

Love to you all

Thank you for listening

Believe in me believe in you

3/3

Chapter 3

Published 5 September 2021

Intention.. I didn't understand that was the key…

I still can't sleep

The answer

Haunts me

The lesson of worthiness

What value do I put upon myself

I'm worth so much

Me the warrior

Only when you

Can back up your beautiful words

With actions

When the door opens

A choice

At least you know the truth

You can strip the heart

Of layers

1/5

Don't speak beautiful words

When your actions

Say otherwise

Makes me feel worthless

Like dirt

A warrior deserves

To be truly loved

Have true love

Not given

Then taken

To have forgiveness

For mistakes made

Not to be mistreated

To fill a gap

In or out

I am worthy of greatness

I'm not perfect

I'm not out to hurt anyone

I'm on this earth to learn

Words that make you feel worthy

Are like daggers

I know now they mean everything

Reality is, Why say it

When you can't live it

It's the truth

But if you say those words

Then take it away

With actions

How much value

Do you put on that person

Dangling a carrot

I've done it again

Being a doormat

If I say something I mean it

Words can hurt

Even the most beautiful

Most inspiring

These could be daggers

The true love you speak

You are worthy, not second place

And you will find that person

Who will give you that, Unconditionally

Each time, Crushing hope

I've been a fool

Once again

This time

I'm nobody's fool

You can do nothing wrong

But you are worthy

I say,

I learnt,

Don't say it

If you can't back it up, 100%

My weight in gold

If this is the final lesson

I have understood it

Leaving my heart open

Is ok

But my heart

Is worthy of being out

Without fear

Of being crushed

At least I'm not living a lie

4/5

Or lying to myself
Or are you
The universal lessons,
Are so different
When you come from a different place
My heart was unlocked
I saw what pure love is
I also felt what it was
To be vulnerable
To have my worth compromised
The warrior is here
Inside me, the greatest lessons are still to come

Chapter 4

Published 8 September 2021

In silence, I have grown the most

On a train….

The Passengers

Look at me.. With caring eyes

I've been a fool

The lesson was right in front of me

The lesson of my self-worth

I know

What do I mean

My eyes say it all

I'm worth so much

My heart that I give out

Every time

I get hurt

But that's because I'm me

One day

I will be chosen

No games

The spirit

Will be your guide

I am worthy and valued

I am better than what I think

I make others happy

I can see that

You will treat them with love

But you know

They will totally idolise you

It might be your truth

A couple say, This is your lesson

But realistically,

Another lesson

Actions and words

Must match on my heart

If I open up again

The couple grab my hands

Warrior you are beautiful, You are the best person

You do everything for everyone

You don't want recognition

You deserve respect

But respect and love you … that's the challenge

Actions speak louder than words

I learnt that

I'm just getting the final lesson

The hardest of them all

I say thank you to the couple

They depart

The universal lessons

Are so different

When you come from a different place

My heart was unlocked

I always do this

I live in Fantasia

Where all is well

I'm still there

I have boundaries

I am worthy of so much more

Lesson completed

For the next time

I go to my waterfall now to cleanse

Chapter 5

Published 12 September 2021

A leader is someone who respects and helps the people that help and gives them more as thanks

New life

Emotions and feelings

Can be scary

The unknown

To us all, Is exciting

Our dreams come close

Also giving up

Yourself, To be guided

It's another scary phase

The train, I ride

This place, I call home

Has been nothing short of magical

Finally I am on the right path

The people

They speak, Say it all

Long and hard

We have given ourselves

Always looking

for a way out

But it was as simple

Simple as letting go

Trusting all emotions

No fear of hurt

No pain,

Embrace it

The good, The painful

We all have our journey

As a warrior, a Healer

I walk this path now

I don't know

What to expect

I'm just looking

Out my window

I hold so dear

This stage of life, That is now

2/3

Must be loved

Loved and enjoyed

The moon sets

The sun rises

My heart is open

I make myself safe

I always will

Thank you for listening

Chapter 6

Published 15 September 2021

You must have the courage to shut the door and walk away

I see it all

Or do I

Actions of others

Mean a lot

But the feeling

Of seeing

The honesty, Within you

Your truth

Means everything, Until proven

We see

All around

The faces, The people

The words muttered

Are they speaking

From fear

Or their truth

Whatever It may be

Be honest

When you know

Inside

You've been lied to

Used

Now your guard is up

Your soul, Spirit, Heart

Heavy

You're mind

Racing, thinking

When out of your comfort zone

When money appears

Power is given

They are truly

Backed into a corner

Is it survival

Or is it

The hidden

Secrets, That they hide

We all have them

But you see

Are we selfish

But what is selfish

No one is selfish

Only if you use this

Against others

Hold true

No hurt

Just heal, Yourself

Your family and friends, The world

This is why

Invisibility

Can be good

As a start of the new chapter

Chapter 7

Published 17 September 2021

**When the veil is off
The truth you see is exactly that…
People can't hide it**

My head

My mind spins

My heart races

Lost, Crazy vibes

Scared soul

A crazy train

The fire, So deep

The flames

Open the door

To my soul

Where

I try to find myself

Am I wrong

To speak

About the hurt, the pain

The stabbing

Goes deeper

Understanding all strikes,

Cause pain

To get up….Its hard

As a person

Only acceptance

We all desire

The words

Do I love me

I say it

Do I believe it

I give

Without reward

When I need

Why am I

The invisible person

Until screams

The voice is heard

As I fall

Tired, Drained

Emotionally scarred

Now, It's my time

For me

And only me

The stars align

I sit here

I have always wanted

I give too much

Why

the ego said,

as I say defeated in hope

yes, ok

I hope not

I lay to rest

To wake

Another day

Thank you for listening

Chapter 8

Published 27 September 2021

I think of the way that society and its standards impact you and your life. Awareness is great, at least you check your self and check your ego at the door

I saw this

This sums up why I create

What makes me

I can't cope these days

Negativity, Low Vibration

No harm to others

But also

No harm to me

People I know deep down

Effected by ego and money

I have been influenced

My life is an escape now

from the pain

1/2

It's not wanted,

But it's there

to heal is to accept and

move forward with what you love

The human race

can be so cruel in a lot of ways

No one really gets anyone in a lot of cases

There's the treatment of an individual

that turns them into someone else

They have had enough, or they need to be protected

Really only rely on myself

Just a thought, a message

Chapter 9

Published 2 October 2021

The storm in your mind …
the fight that is needless

We stand

Loving life

When hurt

We crawl

Defensive about the world

People Saying

you did this

You did that

It's hurting me

The pain only I can feel

We are either

A victim

Or a subconscious demon

That raises his head,

from the depths

The voices say to me..

You hurt me

I feel like this

You contributed

You'll pay

Acknowledging this

Is the first step

To a better life

Two parties

Three parties

The ego flying

Must be loving

The self-destruction

I'm learning

Trauma

Held inside

Enhances battle

Tailspin, a Tornado

The real people

That hurt you

Walk away

They say become stronger

Don't let that hurt you

Easier said

No one knows

The scars

People leave

In pain

We react

We adore

We are hit hard

The person

overtaken the soul

Your greatest battle

It takes an angel

To withstand that

And a warrior

To stand up again

Each hit I take

I take longer to rise

To forgive

Not forget

But not let it In

To control you

Each minute

Each second

You're fears

Come forth

You scream

Inside

Your chest

Sinks

Your eyes

Tell the story of battle

I've held in

Not let go

I explode

It takes over

Where to escape

The closest people

You hope

Will assist you

And forgive

Others, the enemies that hurt you

Knowing

Your struggles

Knowing your heart

Is bleeding

Your spirit

Cracked

Deep down

The warrior is dead

Just being responsible

Saying sorry

Should be enough

But it's not

Am I'm wrong

Because

I didn't get sorry

Truly

From those

Who strangled my soul

Now if I can move on

As I drive

I will be positive

Honest

And not let this

Hinder me

Silence

Acceptance

Turn the back

To these people

Will I save me

Change my scene

The passengers, people I meet

Will help

Like they did before

Ride on

Thank you for listening

Chapter 10

Published 8 October 2021

A truth … a daily pledge to yourself

Actions speak louder than words

I must take my own advice

This will heal me

From the pain

I have been hiding

Been showing me the light

Want to be rid of

The hardest thing

Is controlling the ego

Speaking, I hear the sounds

You've been wronged

Make a statement

You owe it, to me

Let's do this

A great honour to be apart of Poizonus in Tasmania

With Eagles Brownlow Medalist Benny Cousins and Benji MIlls

Meeting my WASP Family of the USA Blind in Texas 2024

4 amazing friends living the dream

Japan Temples 2024

Hart Family Dungeon

Over 20 years of friendship with this bloke, I am Paul Whitelaw

Charity fundraising with Julian James

Meeting the next big thing Roman Reigns, 2015

Meeting WCW Champ Sting, 1998

Chapter 11

Published 15 October 2021

Silence speaks volumes

Words of the Warrior

To unlock your Acana

You must go deep within

The deepest darkest secrets, must be tackled heads on

Once accepted,

Your purpose will come forth.

Chapter 12

Published 22 October 2021

Trust in the flow
It will be the greatest decision you will make

Words

Powerful

When spoken

What is the meaning

Why is it said

For the reason

Only one knows

Fear

Love

To make a point

Are they listening

I am

They resonate

Inside my mind

Forgive

Always

But not forget

Words

Verbal actions

With my words

Have hurt people

Yes

Felt regret

Yes

When the spear

Of words

Come to me

Imbed inside

No one

Truly understands

When said

In your heart

In your mind

It finds a home

Until, the time comes to leave

Forever

Chapter 13

Published 28 October 2021

Dis-ease, is when your gut talks to you

Leaving a sign

Not to forget

But to understand

Becoming better

Looking wider

Deeper

Into why it's said

No excuse

That's a choice

I have

Made the turn

Walked forward

Walked away

Anytime

With my power

That is sacred

The Train I drive

I love you

What you stand for

You are the making

Of the real me

The balance I need

My guides

The symbolic figures

That watch over my spirit

Remind me, Each day, Why I breathe

Thank you for listening

Chapter 14

Published 1 November 2021

Words can be the greatest healer, but also the greatest source of hurt

Once stranded

Alone

Looking ahead

To nothing

A hole

A rage inside

Why does this fire burn

Am I feeling wronged

Or am I, the one

Who is wrong

In the mirror

I see me

Or was it pain

If me

Finding me
Believing in me
Others don't count
If they ask
The idol inside
To change
I believe
I see two parts
To every story
Each has its own ending
Its own meaning
I say the power
What does it mean
In each of us
It's our spirit
To once we live
Broken
Can be mended
But unstable
To be hurt
Once again

2/3

Like a warrior

We get up

Again

Once again

Until

No more

Chapter 15

Published 10 November 2021

Trying is a good word, action is the greatest victory

A verse from me ….. Wild horses let be free

You must be in balance

Embrace the light

Embrace the dark

The angels

The so called demons

They all resemble

A lesson we can take from

Become your own identity

In this world you are the best you can be

No one can take you down

People who accept you

You'll feel it

They will love you

Regardless

They will help you

Not change you

They will stand by you

As you take the ride

For better or worse

No judgement

Pure support

Wild horse

Run free

The train you ride

Is the journey

That doesn't end

But it is, The greatest ride of your life

Chapter 16

Published 13th November 2021

You can have a physical connection with someone but what does it mean when emotions come into play.

Words of the Warrior

It takes strength and courage to move on

To step away from a love

To choose you, will be one of your greatest victories.

Even though at the time

It feels like heartbreak

Chapter 17

Published 14 November 2021

Alone, a word that means finding yourself

I wish for better

Or just looking

For light

I walked yesterday

Finding true balance

Is my saviour

It will happen

Everything

Happens for a reason

The message

Starting at me

I just

Have to take it

With both hands

Losing power

Giving away

For no reason

I'm a helper, I like helping

I see light

Just helping

Healing

Fellow humans

I must, It part of me

Look in the mirror

To remember

The person

looking at me

Needs help too

Don't forget

I won't

Keep enthusiastic

Watch for vampires

Protect that light

That shines so bright

I have the power

My greatest strength

Each day
Remind yourself
Of your life force
Find your purpose
Your identity
And you
The Train ride
Thank you

3/3

Chapter 18

Published 26 November 2021

Anger is an emotion, being cruel is an action of anger …

On your way

To your home

Don't be afraid to look back

See where you come from

It may be scary

But it's good to see where you come from

You will be so proud of yourself

Chapter 19

Published 6 December 2021

Greatest statement is when you step away

I still can't sleep

The answer

Haunts me

The lesson of worthiness

What value

Do I put upon myself

I'm worth so much

Me the warrior

Only when you

Can back up your beautiful words

With the appropriate actions

When the door opens

A choice

At least you know the truth

You can strip the heart

Of layers

Don't speak beautiful words

When you're actions

Say otherwise

Makes me feel worthless

Like dirt

The warrior deserves

To be truly loved

Have true love

Not given

Then taken

Chapter 20

Published 10 December 2021

Take it with both hands .. with love

A message

In the morning light

As the train whistle blows

To have forgiveness

For mistakes made

Not to be mistreated

To fill a gap

In or out

That's because

I am worthy of greatness

Today is here

The passengers

Look at me

With blank faces

A young couple say

How are you warrior

I reply

I've been a fool

The lesson was right in front of me

The lesson of my self worth

They ask

I say

I'm worth so much

My heart that I give out

Every time, But that's because I'm me

I'm not perfect

I'm not out to hurt anyone

I'm on this earth to learn

Chapter 21

Published 25 December 2021

Your purpose, is within your soul.. look deep and don't be afraid to release it

Upon this day

I look at the sky

I see pain, heartbreak and sadness

I also see hope, joy and abundance

It's a choice on what I focus on

The pain will be the lesson

Finding that purpose

Will be your greatest gift

You can see the light, the goal

The happiness your heart has always desired

Steve and Sahara

Meeting Felipe, Jim and Bill, The Village People 2014

Sahara and I meeting Damien Bodie from Winners and Losers, 2010

Team PI tag champs

Ursala, "The Trevor", Jaylee and me

First Photo on my world trip 2024 with Grace

A proud DDPY instructor at Mind Body Spirit Festival 2018 with German Silva

A summers day at Lake Louise Canada

Cosplaying The Fiend Bray Wyatt (RIP)

Flying the aussie flag at AEW Dynamite 3rd of July 2024

Fun times at Calgary Stampede with Evan and Tyla 2024

Gary's 40th Dress up with our friend Coby Gray R.I.P (Fred Flinstone)

Chapter 22

Published 26 December 2021

A White flame ... the purest of power

It's how we react

our next move

walk or sit

channelling

our inner power

Expression is what we must

Embrace mine

To be wanted

To have self-trust

Proving myself

Only to me

Messages of good vs bad

Positive vs Negative

Light vs Dark

within us

We battle for balance

Experiencing each emotion

I can be

A warrior for light

A magician of my world

A healer to all

I don't wish

Any bad on anyone

Have a great life

But I will too

Without toxic energy vampires

Chapter 23

Published 1 January 2022

First step is like the winds of change…

I am not any better than anyone

But I am justice…..for me

It's a right to be … but so will I

Be yourself

Be proud

Send love to you, then others

If you can't love you

The flame can't ignite with full force

Negativity, I blast with white light

The greatest

True

Pure love

We all can't be close

we can love ourselves and those in our tribe

Chapter 24

Published 10 January 2022

Holding your hand
Your rock
When you need

Doubt

Has been my enemy

I see

I said

I can't, It's too hard

Why?

Because of others

Saying you can't

I believed them

That's the way

The voice in my head

Keeps speaking

That little voice

1/3

In my heart

Saying

You can

You're worthy

You're strong

Don't fear

Just walk

Failure

Is not real

It's a lesson

A teacher

I sit here

Looking at all I've done

Accomplished

The reason I sit here

I have it all

Inside of me

Nowhere else

But to be inspired

Being truly believed in

2/3

Is beautiful

A dream

A want

I've had

Is mine

Chapter 25

Published 17 January 2022

Some demons may come back to haunt you …

I feel a presence

My heart

My chest becomes tight

I feel heavy

I have been injected

With energetic poison

The past

Coming

To interrupt

My present

The greatest fight

Feelings

Guilt

Sadness

Sorrow

Regret

Innocence lost

My greatest battle

To fight

When attacked

Flame is on

Two forces

Hitting

I've been here before

I'm tired

I can't

But I have too

For me and my soul family

Chapter 26

Published 21 January 2022

The greatest gift someone will give you is the key to their soul

Battle after battle

This could end it

But I must win

Over all

I will win

This is my life

No one else's

I make mistakes

If I have hurt people

I'm sorry

But if you love me

Then forgive

As I won't

Be a person

That continually

Bows for mistakes made

Continual reminders

Need to cease

Healing needs to begin

White Flame alight

I will

I won't falter

Sometimes

Life is a battle

Pick them

To fight

If it's really worth it

This feeling

In my heart

I've had before

No more

Repeated strikes

I yield once

I accept

Then we heal together

As the powers of the spirits before me

The animals, that have guarded me

Send whitelight

To victory

Love and peace

As one

3/3

Chapter 27

Published 27 January 2022

**Being Vulnerable, and truly Honest without fear ….
Just remember its like riding a bike, you will fall off
and get hurt**

A day in the sun… let the water speak

The power

That comes from above

Most people don't truly

Understand

I sit here

Contemplating

What has happened

What is about to come

The flames alight

As normal

The plants are talking

To heal

Physically

Emotionally

To connect again

I place my hand

Is the cool springs

Splash, On my face

Told to relax

Sit back

You deserve it

I am

What I need to be

A new chapter

Surreal

In some cases

Dreams

The messages

The light

That shines upon us

It's now

It's here

We are one

Now to enjoy

2/3

Less worry

Take care of me

No excuses

In every way

I have it all

I had it all

I just needed

Someone to truly believe

In me, that power

You can't explain

Take care my friend

Chapter 28

Published 9 February 2022

Protect your vibration, your flow and your smile

We hear

We hold

So many thoughts

Emotions

Love

Anger

Frustration

When it wants

It comes out

It takes

Such a person

With strength

Courage

To show

Vulnerability

But it takes

A greater person

To be by your side

In your time of need

You don't change

You still are you

Storms

Thunder

Lightening

Won't move me

Helpless

Yes maybe

But a quiet person

In your time

Of need

I'll be there for you

These 5 words I say to you

When I breathe

I want to be the air for you

Been a song

We have all heard

As I walk another day

Chapter 29

Published 23 February 2022

Life is like the circus, lots of different acts and fun for you to enjoy

The power

That comes from above

Most people don't truly

Understand

I sit here

Contemplating

What has happened

What is about to come

The shadow will take me

To the new frontier

A new life

The one that I always dreamed of

Chapter 30

Published 7 March 2022

You are the diamond, you always wanted.

When it wants

It comes out

It takes

Such a person

With strength

Courage

To show everything I need

When I go through the forbidden door

The key was given to me

But we turned it

I walked through

It was scary

It hurt so much

But with that hurt

Comes courage, strength and a new life

Embrace it

I hope others will follow my lead

Be Vulnerable

Be real

Be you and find your purpose

Embrace your soul

Find that true

Chapter 31

Published 10 March 2022

Success is all about the work you do

Being ruled

By the moon

The power

Upon me

Is intense

How do I control

The emotions

Let them override me

Lash out

Just with emotion

Not vicious

But I'm not happy

I reflect

I feel

The past

It will be a part of me

But I do learn

Appreciate

Feel low

When I let

These emotions

These people

Control me

I have to be better

I must

To be a greater soul

A peaceful soul

I must be better

I will be better

Unfortunately

We live in turmoil

And we must

Ride the wind

But knowledge

Acceptance

And willing

2/3

To change

To be better

Love wins

Always

A dream

A want

I've had

Is mine

Grand Final Day 2018 with Sahara-Rose

Live Wild Child WASP Australia in Sydney 2024

My beautiful Canadian Family Sarah and Willar

My hero, Bray Wyatt (RIP), Thank you

My little rock

Neighbours backstage 2004 with Yakka and Firestarter (RIP)

Tasmania with these legends, Matty Bee and Poizonus

Meeting Dwayne "The Rock" Johnson

Robin the Boy Wonder of Oz, promo shots in Canada

Red Horse and Myself at Mind Body Spirit Festival 2016

Superheroes raising money for a good cause

Chapter 32

Published 20 March 2022

Being right or being happy… what would you do

Memories arise

People

Places

Incidents

Actions

Some proud

Some I look down

As I walk to the water

I look into the sky

I hear the train

I know that sound

I awake

Every morning

To its power

Why and what

The people

That have affected us

We must forgive

For us

And forget

Release

No contact

No emotion

This is my challenge

After being in a war

With myself

It's human nature

To be drawn

To what you know

I see now

That embrace my life

Hold different promises

Live in harmony

Look into the sky

The moon, The sun

Nothing to prove

Chapter 33

Published 28 March 2022

Look at yourself in the mirror and say "Ï love you" .. how does it make you feel?

The moment

Is what we wait for

The moment

When it turns our life

The moment

When it makes us smile

We sigh

In relief

In joy

Our next breath

Is the best one

We will take

As we connect

Once again

To spirit

To realign

With our guides

When you feel

The path is clear

I see the white flames

That surround me

Protect me

On this journey, I take the walk

Vulnerable

Love opens up

A heart, that was chained

Holding down

Life is a new chapter

Enjoy it

Chapter 34

Published 29 March 2022

You really don't owe anyone anything, you give a gift because you are grateful

White Flame

That is your name

"White Flame"

A symbol

Of a warrior

A healer

A magician

A protector

Be you

What are you here for

What's been in your heart

Heed our words

The guides speak

Take this journey

Leave behind

The baggage

Send love

As you do

Walk to Oz

With the ones you love

Flora

Fauna

The animals

Guides god and the angels

We are here

You will walk

You will need reminding

Don't lose track

Keep connected

I place my head

Onto Mother Earth

I mutter, Quietly

The words, Thank you

For the honour

Of being named

"White Flame"

I will only do my best

Not perfect

But with an loving heart

And soul

I thank you

I walk back

We stand, As one

And start, Walking to Oz

Chapter 35

Published 15 April 2022

I am sure people really don't listen to what I say, or they don't let me finish

I feel the chill

The ice

Upon my nose

The wind howls

I turn

No one there

Chest is tightening

With anticipation

Fear

Even A little frustration and anger

Why I say

Show yourself

Let me feel

Your fury and wrath

I have know

Each time

Mother Earth asks

Hold me

Flame on

White flame warrior

The most powerful

The most powerful

White lighter

Surround yourself

In a ball

Of pure white flames

You are untouchable

No one can harm

No storm can stop you

It will push you

Stop you to your knees

Knock you down

But you'll get up

The choice

of walking forward

Instead of staying down

Changes your life

Chapter 36

Published 20 April 2022

Learn to fuel love instead of fear

My soul

My spirit

My heart

We have no choice

I must walk

Be brave

Hold tight

As you do

Your heart

Two souls together

True love can conquer all

The white flame

Is pure love

The storm

Starts to cease

The light comes through

The endless pursuit

Is over

I thank her

I hold her hand and continue

To my dream, our dream

I awake, with a smile

Chapter 37

Published 26 April 2022

Bikes, cars and trains, we learn to drive them, we need to remember to learn to drive ourselves

The greatest threat

The fear inside

Can be defeated

I felt this

Being on the train

Prepares you

Teaches you

To be strong

For that moment

For me

The desire

The want

To be truly loved

Feelings

1/2

So many

I know

Turning

To white light

The white flame warrior

Pure love

For me

Is here

The words

Spoken so true

I know

The guides

Are smiling

The wolf sits, contented

Chapter 38

Published 23 April 2022

"Own your sh**, but remember people have to own theirs as well, including treating you with disrespect. Maintain your integrity and set new boundaries that people who love you will respect

The Feelings of you

Go up and down

Like a roller coaster

Words

Can't describe

How I felt

This warrior

Just became

Immortal

Inside

Nothing

Will erase this feeling

Thank you

You truly started my healing

My angel

My life

My soulmate

Our hearts

As one, Stronger

More powerful

The greatest gift

The greatest power

True love, that does conquer all

Chapter 39

Published 3 May 2022

It's a choice to change your thinking

When I hear that voice

It changes my world

I'm free

I smile

My heart grows

The magnet

Another half

A soul connection

You truly feel the energy

I can't explain

But it's more

More than anything I felt

I've grown

I've learnt

I've been through the tornado

But I'm here

I'm where I am meant to be

A touch, connection of energies

The Protector

Even when

Apart

Our souls are one

Irrepressible , Unbelievable

Nothing you can describe

Only knowing

After the journey

To have hurt, the loss

Ready to fight

Chapter 40

Published 21 May 2022

The universe .. my friend … my teacher ….. finding Oz

I gave to many

My heart

My trust

My soul

To be liked

Acceptance

I got hurt

I built up

The guard

No one enters

I close my eyes

I feel the energy

The hand

On the gate

On my heart

Scared, yes

I wanted to run

Is it the words I wished

The ones

I desperately want to hear

In my dreams

A heart of gold

Strength and courage

True

Pure

Hope

Is the word

When heard

That ignites my deepest dreams

Ones I kept

Under lock and key

I feel it

I push it away

For so long now

A true heart

Wins always

When the time is right

When you have learnt the lesson

If let go

If I am me again

I am your protector

Your one love

I must trust

I give my heart

Not my power

My trust

I give you me

As you give me you

Take me as I am

or just walk away

When I walk to Oz

A dream

A message

I've had for so long

With you

As me

3/3

Team PI" 3 Time Aussie Tag Champs

The amazing Trio of Ox, Julian and Stephan

The Arse Villains BIg Daddy, Stephan Cool and RIP Firestarter

Crazy times, just like WASP at Shinjuku Catcus Club Japan

Kent, the owner of Shinjuku Cactus Club, Japan

The Rocket Owen Harts Grave, Calgary Canada

Two men with a beautiful friendship

The WASP Family, Malicky and Kyo

Village People Indian, Felipe 2014

Robin protecting Vancouver Canada

WWH Journey of a Whitefeather

Dreaming of winning Dancing with the Stars

Best times and Best times with the wrestling family

My Wrestling Family

Meeting Paula Abdul at the Logies

My friend I miss you SCreaming Lord Lush RIP

Off to the crazy Steel Panther concert in Sydney with Lyndall

The Widowmaker live at Wrestlerock

Chapter 41

Published 24 May 2022

Ego speaks when you do something that you'd love to tell the world. I know now, It's better just to have a party of one

I write this when I was there…

Well I thought I was

Maybe I was

For the vibration and mindset I was at the time

One thing it says

True emotion writes the best entries…

I might be away from you

But I know my heart is always with you

Your heart is always within me

You're always next to me spiritually and that's what

true love is

I know that now

You taught me how to love

To love myself

To let my guard down

Fear is gone

Love and lots of it

Will and does conquer

Anything

You

Me

We are one

But we are ourselves

Our own people

But our hearts are one

Thank you

Our future

I know

Is blessed with white light

It will be

Everything we want

These words I say

Becoming the white magician

Creator of my world

It's now

Pure whitelight

Over my body

The symbol of goodness

The symbol of my strength

The journey has started

I've earned it

We all earn it

Chapter 42

Published 3 June 2022

All things end, its sad, but then a new book can be opened

Love is special

Something that I let in

Regardless of how and when

I'm vulnerable

I didn't give up

I just want to bury the past

We only live for a short time

Not many people experience this

It's true

It genuine

It's real

It's also scary

I know that's where my mind is

Even through the rain

I won't give up

1/2

Even though I might go through a

hurricane myself

I'm here for you

Forever and always

In saying that

My heart

Even though vulnerable

Will always have a boundary that will

protect it

I've been through too much

Hope you can understand

In time I know you will

Because one day

Nothing will matter

Let's make sure

That the worlds

We live in

Are filled with love

As it should be

Chapter 43

Published 6 June 2022

Outside Behaviours, don't effect you unless you let them

I say these words
The meaning
holds true
I close my eyes
On this day
In this hour
I call upon the ancient power
The White Flame
That engulfs my soul
I ask thee
To send my trust
Within my heart
To believe
To honour
To be me
I am the person
That is coming out

The shadows
where I dwelled
I say goodbye
Nothing less
than full Happiness
The light that shines
From my heart
The white light
The white flame
The power of good
That sees me
Build, create, protect and Heal
I say this in this moonlight
The water that flows
I see and sit
You are the new world
My real world
The flame I walk in
The white flame
Love powers all

Chapter 44

Published 30 June 2022

Messages come to me …open to the white flame

Being connected

Deeper

Higher consciousness

Means we see

We feel

Learn to cope

With life

Is it easy

No

But we take it back

To the ones we love

A message

Came to me

In the moment

I say this

"You're my everything sweetheart"

I love you like no other

When you're in pain

I can feel it in my heart

Our hearts are one

But our love is the strongest thing on

This planet, we can't be broken, always and forever

Chapter 45

Published 2 July 2022

Success is all about the work you do

I walk stronger

I must be better

Learning each day

That it means more

To be you

But your here

On this earth

Surround yourself

With your tribe

No harm to others

They are your saviours

The chance to breath

To be you

To learn

To be better

Spiritual forgiveness

Is a gift

Like wild horses

Be free

I thank you

Chapter 46

Published 11 July 2022

Sometimes you wonder why people love animals over the human race, it's quite sad, but I get it

I see messages

On the screens

I see memories

That I cringe

Remind me of times past

Of fear

Scared

Being alone

Having to think

What's next

Can't change it

But it lays dormant

What do I fear

Failure

Not any more

Being hurt

Emotionally

Being reassured

Not having that comfort

When you get it

You crave it

You protect it

You hold it close

It's like a drug

What clicks our mind

To feel like this

To protect

Our heart

It's been broken

Let down

Too many times

I can't dwell

I know

I'm better

But I have my times

And

I know when I'm doing it

I will be better

And take my lessons

From the deepest hurt

It's my only life

Chapter 47

Published 21 July 2022

Remember, you don't know when your time is up

To be loved

Not to be turned on

I feel it more

As that child

Walking lonely

Inside me

Looking for that group

To accept

A person

Who is different

Just to fit in

Truly be **a part** of something

To be one of them

Accepted for me

Not for return

Just for love

But to trust

It's pure

Coming

From the heart

I must forgive

Truly believe

Me

I'm ok

Be brave

Lies hurt

The mask I put on

The path I went down

Hard times

I'm tired

I lay upon the earth

I know

I don't want this uncertainty

In my mind

It's better

But it's all me

I will be the white flame

Chapter 48

Published 31 July 2022

Everybody is out for themselves, it's just the way they treat others on the way to their Oz ….

Do not expecting anything

You will get hurt

Knowing

I bring it on myself

Not protecting me

I will now

Forgive

Yes

Forget

Not

Warrior

I am

A little boy

Wanting

Maybe I am
The invisible boy
Who wants to be seen
As I grow I know I can see
When I look into the mirror
The mirror
I see
That invisible boy
The mirror speaks,
Say it's ok
Say thank you
You were strong
My hero
I will be there for us

Chapter 49

Published 12 August 2022

The mirror, will tell you all, just take the time to listen

Sitting

Connecting

Spiritually

With Mother Earth

Going deep

To that cage

That corner

I have been hiding

Where I run

The darkness

The lonely plains

As I look

Deep into the flames

The keys

Given to me

Open the cage

To face the demons

Adult me

Looks into the past

We must heal

The memories, The pain

The answers heard

What I want, Deep down inside

The adult

Looking

To comfort

The fallen soul

The inner child

That is hurt

It consumes

My being

I shouldn't

I need to heal

Be my own doctor

Look after this child

Say it's ok

The inner child

The scared boy

Doesn't speak

Just lies there

Says it's ok

But it's not

For him

3/3

Chapter 50

Published 24 August 2022

Opinions are like a********, everyone has one

For me

I give a lot

I don't receive

That care

The true care

I have blocked

The feelings

I don't speak up

Even now

Being the voice

The boy didn't have

You must let you

I must let go

I say

Yes

But I must stand up

Stop the hurt

Still holding on

Why

I'm done

With the constant hurt

Constant negativity

That fuels

Fear

Resentment

Lowers tolerance

To me

I maybe wrong

People take advantage

Not being called out

But I know

I let this happen

As I don't know

How to control

The power that takes me

I ponder

The thoughts

Exhausting

Staying relevant

On this earth

Fighting myself

Or am I

Talking

To my past self

The invisible boy

Always screaming inside

Doing anything

To be someone

To find love

To be told

You matter

Just you

Not anything you have

Just what's inside

To move on

The child

Must be taught

3/4

By me

You're safe

Ride with me

No one will hurt you

It's ok

You can be you

Dear child

You've been through enough

By yourself

You're safe

Learn life and be you

All will be

Each time

Let me lead

I must rest

As now

The new journey begins

Thanks for listening

Acknowledgements

Editor : Peter Symons.

To these people who also took a gave me an opportunity:

Tim, James, Evan, Deb and Adam.

Andy the best broadcaster and sports podcaster, thanks legend.

Thank you, Sahara-Rose my rock, this book is dedicated to you. I love you.

My god son Ryker "Coke", an honour it is.

Wrestling Family: Myall, Frank, Robbie, Daniel, Mark, Luke, Kala, Mike, Scotty, Glenn (PI), Mick, Rodney, Peter, John, Sam, Tyrone, Mitch, Julian, Benny, and Lyndall, Drago, Amanda & Kristy and Family, Kathryn, Ed, George, Con, Adrian and Shelley, George, Gary, Scott, Mike and Jason …. the best friends a person could have.

To Mum and Dad for giving me life.

Thank you to these people who gave me a chance:

Allan, George, Greg, Mark who gave me a chance at the sport I loved.

To my mentor Bernie, thank you for taking a chance on me.

Clive, Kerri, Diedre and Marco, Karen, Zac and family, Eric, Dallas, Craig, Haydn and the DDPY family.

Life teachers and mentors and their support through hard times: Red Horse & Natalia, Greg and Michael.

The Family : Cortez, Diana, Sarah, Jackie and Solomon.

To these people, thank you for being friends:

Graeme, Allie and Pedge, German, Tony and Jenny, Mario, Mark, and Jen, Nicole & Dean , Danny, Jaylee, Cassie, "False Steve" Jase & Cait, David, Michael "Cmon Ian", Rob and Drew, Chrissi and Paul, Darren & Rowan, Jerry and Family, Paul and Family, Benji, Simay, Jim, Anna, Andy, Luke, Con, Georgiana, Trev, Ursala, Marcel, Matty, Dylan, Ange, Corina, Maria, Elio, Diego, Camila, Ron, Rossco, Nash, Nate, Michelle, Lynne and Peter, Evan, Chris, Karen, Robert and Family, Dazzler "Condiments", Damo, Kate, Mark, Andrew, Joe, Steve and, Jimmy, Heath, Wayno (The Pace Car), Shannon, Jarrod, Karen, Justin & Sheryl, David, Claudia and Michael, Kev, Trav, Jacinda, Luna, Kyo, Naofumi, Malicky and all the members of Love Machine Tokyo, Grace, Taylor, Stacey, Carlos, Yiorgs, Marty, Jayden, Wayne, Col, Aldo & Family, Felix, Colin and Kylie, Rhiannon and Benny B

Special mention to Ros, Lisa and Francie.

Go to Sleep
our little friend
Beneath the evening stars
You will always be our friend
No matter where you are....
Love you my friend
See you in the next life,
Thank you for the gift you have given me

Journey of a Whitefeather

"Remove my mask, write my story"

"From Stroke to Motivational Coach"

THE 15 LESSONS

I received when i woke

The F**K up

Written by Jay Stefanson

"Motivational Coach & Holistic Healer'

B.App Sci (Phys.Ed), Dip.Ed, Ad.Dip Hth.Sci (Myotherapy)

Australia's First DDPYoga Instructor

For your free copy of my ebook please email whitewarriorhealth@gmail.com or contact us on social media #journeyofawhitefeather

www.ingramcontent.com/pod-product-compliance
Lightning Source LLC
Chambersburg PA
CBHW062037290426
44109CB00026B/2647